FILIPPO'S DOME

ANNE ROCKWELL

ATHENEUM 1967 NEW YORK

For Oliver

PROLOGUE

IN THE YEAR 1296 THE CITY OF FLORENCE IN ITALY was prosperous and at peace. Her principal church, Santa Reparata, had begun to seem too small for a growing city, and so the citizens decided to tear it down and build a new church.

The commission to build the church was given to the architect Arnolfo di Cambio. Arnolfo was famous; he had built many of the most important palaces and public buildings in Florence, and he was currently in the process of building the turreted walls that were to enclose and protect the city. The cornerstone was laid and blessed with great ceremony in 1296, and it was decided that the new church would be called St. Mary of the Flower.

Arnolfo and his master masons began their work. At times, the poet Dante Alighieri stood in a favorite spot to view the construction work with fascination. And not only Dante, but all of the people believed, with pride, that their cathedral would be the most glorious in the entire world when it was finished.

But the beginning of the fourteenth century brought a gradual end to the happy and prosperous years preceding. Bitter civic quarrels divided the city and these quarrels were followed by wars

abroad. For a few years before Arnolfo's death in 1310, work had slackened on the cathedral, for the funds set aside for its construction were needed to finance armies. After Arnolfo died, work stopped almost completely. He had built the strong foundations and the beautiful side walls and he had designed a plan that could be easily followed by another architect. But nothing more was done.

After many years the government of the city again grew stable and business prospered. So in 1331 the city decided to begin again the work on the long-neglected cathedral. Responsibility for overseeing the work, choosing an architect, and raising the necessary funds was given to the power-

ful Guild of the Art of Wool. Florence was the most important center in Europe for the finishing and dyeing of raw wool, which was then sold to foreign markets, where it was woven into cloth. The Art of Wool immediately began to provide funds for the work by decreeing that every warehouse and shop in Florence should place a certain sum after every sale or purchase in a special box set up in the shop to receive it. In this way, a great deal of money was soon collected. Then, deciding that above all, the architect should be a famous man, they chose the well-known painter, Giotto di Bondone, to complete plans for the cathedral.

Their choice was wise, for Giotto, late in life, was beginning a new career as an architect, and he now turned all of his skill and imagination to the cathedral. He continued work upon Arnolfo's walls and built the graceful bell tower, which was an accompanying but separate part of the cathedral. Then in 1337 Giotto died, and after this work and progress again fell off.

In 1348 a ship from the Eastern Mediterranean docked at Pisa. Someone aboard was ill and the illness rapidly spread from person to person throughout the warm towns of Tuscany. By the time the disease reached Florence, it had become a greater terror than people of that time had ever known. The illness was the terrible bubonic plague and it meant almost instant death. The storyteller Giovanni Boccaccio has left us a vivid and frightening description of its effect on Florence, and he tells us that in that one hot and humid summer of 1348, more than one hundred thousand people in Florence died. Normal life collapsed; people abandoned property and loved ones and fled to the cooler hills, in the often vain hope that they could there escape the plague.

The plague continued to rage throughout that whole summer, but with the coming of autumn, it had run its course and people once again returned to their homes. Life began again, and to those who had been spared it seemed more precious for having been so nearly lost. Many survivors wished to give thanks to God for sparing them. One tangible way they could do this was to give generously to the church. Then, too, many who had died had willed all of their property to the church. Thus, although the city was desolated and dwarfed, the unfinished church of St. Mary of the Flower had new riches for its construction.

Florence recovered rapidly from the catastrophe, and the old plans of Arnolfo, prepared sixty years earlier, seemed inadequate. People were sure that Florence would soon be greater than before the plague, and they believed that the cathedral should be vastly enlarged to meet future needs.

The width would remain the same, but the walls were to be made twenty-one feet higher, and the length was to be increased by one-third. This work was entrusted to a man named Francesco Talenti, an architect of whom we know very little. He enlarged the existing church, strengthened the foundation, and began work upon unfinished parts of the church.

A Christian church of this period followed in its ground plan the shape of a cross. There are many variations on the cross plan. The long part of the cross, however, is always called the nave. Aisles may, or may not, run down on either side. This is the part of the church that houses the worshippers. At the head of the cross, at the farthest end of the church, lies the apse. It is here that the altar is placed. Between the nave and the apse the cross shape is formed by two arms extending out at right angles to the nave. Each of these arms, or transepts as they are called, usually houses one or more chapels. At the crossing of the nave by the transepts it was often the practice to heighten the ceiling by means of a dome. In all plans that had ever existed for the church of St. Mary of the Flower, it was intended that a dome would cover this crossing. However, when the extension of Arnolfo's plan was made by Talenti, no explanation of how the resulting greater space should be

7

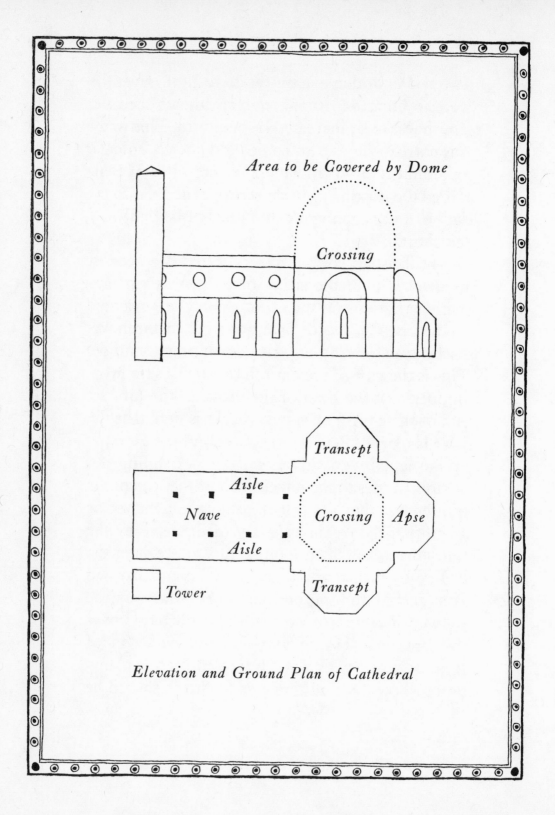

Area to be Covered by Dome

Crossing

Transept

Aisle

Nave   Crossing   Apse

Aisle

Tower

Transept

Elevation and Ground Plan of Cathedral

covered by a dome seems to have been given. A dome such as was called for by the new space was a technical feat that had not been attempted since ancient Roman times. A smaller dome, technically feasible at the time, would have been out of scale and proportion to the new building.

Different architects worked sporadically on the church after Francesco Talenti, but no major construction was done. When the fifteenth century began, the great space over the crossing was unroofed, seemingly forever. Since this was the holiest and most important end of the church, the entire church remained unconsecrated and unused for worship. The problem defied everyone; in all the land there seemed to be no one capable of constructing the dome. The citizens were unhappy with the situation for they were proud of their city and disappointed that her principal monument should have reached such an impossible impasse.

But among the Florentines there was a young goldsmith named Filippo Brunelleschi. He, like so many others, often looked up at the great walls and wondered over and over again if the problem were really insolvable as was said. And as he wondered, he doubted.

I

FILIPPO BRUNELLESCHI WAS THE SON OF A WELL-to-do notary in Florence. His father acted as attorney to many of the professional soldiers of the time, and managed their business affairs. He taught his son to read and write and know arithmetic. Then, because he expected that Filippo would be a notary like himself, he saw to it that the boy read many books on many subjects. However, from his earliest childhood Filippo showed a great interest in drawing pictures. His father, wishing him to be happy and successful in his profession, therefore apprenticed him to a goldsmith.

To be a goldsmith in Florence was a most demanding profession. Only the very gifted were privileged to make things of precious jewels and metals, and they were expected to add greatly, by their art, to the value of the already precious materials they worked with. They made jewels, armor, clocks, coins and numerous other objects, all of which were embellished with magnificent engraved drawings and relief carvings. No art school has since existed that was a better place to develop the minds, eyes, and hands of young artists.

Filippo rapidly mastered the goldsmith's many skills. He was fascinated with weights and bal-

ances, and invented and made some very ingenious watches and alarm clocks, which kept perfect time. And once, for one of the many religious festivals that the Florentines held, he built a device that was the joy and talk of the city.

He cast a metal globe, round like the moon, and left the inside hollow. In this cavity he placed a clockwork mechanism that guided the movement of two rings of angel statues, which spun around the globe in two different orbits. At a given moment a statue of the Archangel Gabriel himself flew out of a little door in the globe. He was contained in a small, almond-shaped vehicle and he joined the host of angels as they spun around and around. So lovely and delightful was this, that when it passed through the streets on a float, the people liked it better than any of the other spectacles that the festival had to offer, and they spoke fondly of their clever Filippo and his fine mechanics.

It was quite natural as time passed for Filippo to turn from the small, precious objects of the goldsmith to the more monumental works of the sculptor. He soon mastered the art of sculpture and developed a powerful and original style. Before long, he was well known for this also.

But as he worked at being a goldsmith and sculptor, he dreamed of one day making buildings. For to Filippo it seemed as if architecture was the mother of all the related arts of painting, sculpture and decoration—and as such, surpassed them.

Architecture is the making of buildings that are large enough for men to move in freely and that are at the same time beautiful and expressive. Although an architect's buildings are visible, basically his art is abstract, as music is, for it pleases and talks to us only by the way it shapes empty space into form.

There are three important spaces to deal with in architecture. The first of these is the flat, or two-dimensional space, which is the wall as a unit. How and where windows, doors and decorations are placed to create a pattern on a flat wall is akin to the pattern a painting makes. The second space is the whole shape that the building forms on the outside: how the roof outlines against the sky, how parts of the building extend outward or recede inward. This space is three-dimensional, like that of the sculptor. The third space is that formed inside the building. It is the rhythm and harmony created by the length of the building, or a part of it, contrasted against the height, and the progressions from room to room and wall to wall. This space is, furthermore, not only a space to look at, as are the other two, but a space to move in, be enclosed by and part of. It is a space formed only by architecture.

An architect looks for ways to make all of these spaces work together to make the whole building beautiful. His problems are complex and difficult, for besides creating beauty, he must also make his building structurally sound, so that it will not fall down. He does this through engineering, the science of knowing the laws of balance and stress and practical building techniques that hold buildings together.

Filippo thought a good deal about all of these things. He watched masons and builders at their work whenever he could. He also heard wonderful things about the great knowledge that the an-

cient Roman builders had had. He was part of a group of people in Florence who read and studied everything they could about ancient Rome. These people—scholars, artists, poets, philosophers, nobles and businessmen—believed that this earlier civilization had been, in many ways, superior to their own. Filippo had occasionally seen Roman coins, which often had images of great Roman temples and other buildings stamped upon them. To Filippo these seemed more magnificent than any modern building he had ever seen, and he longed to see them in reality. Unfortunately, Rome lay many miles to the south of Florence, and Filippo had never had occasion or opportunity to go there.

During the day Filippo worked hard at being a goldsmith and sculptor, but in the evenings, when work was done, he drew pictures of the buildings around him in order to learn how they were put together. He paid special attention to the eleventh century Baptistery of St. John. From this and other beautiful buildings, he learned many things by thoughtful observation. And like most of the citizens of Florence, he thought about the unfinished church of St. Mary of the Flower—the church that people considered doomed to remain unfinished. As he looked up at its gaily decorated marble walls, he tried to imagine a great dome capping the crossing, rising higher than the brown hills that surrounded Florence. In the back of his mind a dream was beginning to grow. This dream was to find a way to raise the dome of St. Mary of the Flower. But because he had no idea yet of how this could be accomplished, he sensibly mentioned it to no one.

In 1401, when Filippo was twenty-four years old, the magistrates of the city decided that the lovely old Baptistery of St. John, across from the cathedral needed a new pair of doors. These doors were to be enormous, made of bronze, and decorated with relief panels telling stories from the Bible. In Florence there were many excellent sculptors. The magistrates were not certain as to who could best do the scenes, so they decided to hold a competition and give the commission as a prize to the winner. It was probably the most important commission any sculptor would receive in his whole lifetime, and many hoped to be the one chosen. But the magistrates limited the competition to six sculptors, of their own choosing, whom they considered to be the best in Florence. Among the six competitors were Filippo and a young man named Lorenzo Ghiberti.

Each of the competitors was given the same Old Testament story to depict in a bronze panel. The scene was to show Abraham about to sacrifice his son, Isaac, but being prevented from this by an angel. Each man worked hard at making his model.

First the figures were modeled roughly in clay, and then the clay was covered with a layer of beeswax, which was carved in greater detail. When the

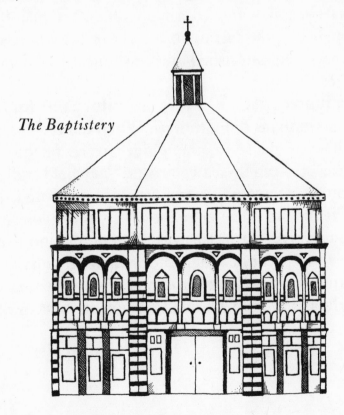

The Baptistery

wax was just as the artist wanted it, "gates," or sticks of solid beeswax, were attached at several points. The entire work was then covered with liquid plaster, which hardened. Once the plaster was hard, or "set," the whole thing was placed in an oven; the wax then melted and ran out through the gates. In its place was a perfect impression of the work, between the clay core and the plaster. Now molten bronze was carefully poured into the gates that the wax had run out of. When the bronze had cooled and hardened, the plaster was cracked away. Inside there was a relief casting, just like the wax, but made of bronze. To finish the bronze relief, the sculptors had only to file and "chase" away the gates and repair any accident that had happened in the casting. Then the entire piece was burnished and polished until it shone with a warm lustre.

Filippo produced a very beautiful panel for the competition, as did Ghiberti. When the time came to make a decision, the judges were unable to choose between these two artists. They held endless discussions, but no matter how they debated the merits of one piece over the other, they were unable to agree. At last it was obvious that no decision would ever be reached, for each artist had his own strong-minded champions who were unable to admit that their choice was not the best. Since someone had to do the doors, and neither Filippo nor Ghiberti seemed to be more competent than the other, the judges at last decided to offer the commission jointly to both men and so declared them both the winner.

However, Filippo did not want to work this way. He believed that one person should have the authority to make the statues as he wished, that this would make the doors most beautiful. More important, he felt, in looking at Ghiberti's well-made piece, that it was superior to his own. For Filippo had cast his panel in several pieces and welded them together later, but Ghiberti had so mastered the art of lost-wax casting that he had cast his entire panel in one piece. He had retained in the bronze all of the subtle delicacy of modeling that the original wax had had.

To come out second best, as Filippo believed he had done, was discouraging. He realized that as a sculptor he had more than met his match, and that furthermore his chief rival was a man four years younger than himself. For Filippo it seemed to be a time for taking stock of himself and his hopes, and it was after the competition for the Baptistery doors had been settled that Filippo's daydreams about the Roman ruins began to turn into something more.

Some say that at first Filippo only thought of

making the trip to Rome in order to see and study antique sculpture. But others say that he made the important decision to go to Rome in order to teach himself the lost arts of Roman architecture. In this way he planned to surpass Ghiberti as he believed architecture surpassed sculpture.

Filippo had inherited a little farm in the olive-covered hills outside of Florence. He sold this farm, and the sale gave him a substantial enough sum of money to live simply in Rome for some time.

At this time he had a good friend who was an apprentice in Ghiberti's workshop, named Donato, or Donatello, as he was called by nearly everyone who knew him. Many times Filippo and Donatello had walked through the crowded streets, bought their lunch of cool white wine, sausages and hard-boiled eggs, and heard none of the commotion surrounding them, because they were talking of Rome. Donatello was young, about fourteen years old, but his enthusiasm for sculpture and his desire to see the sculpture in Rome was enormous. He had heard of marvelous statues of Roman ladies and gentlemen, children and animals, so expressive and realistic that they seemed almost ready to speak and breathe.

And so Filippo, knowing that Donatello would enjoy the journey as much as he, and wanting a companion, invited Donatello to join him. Donatello accepted enthusiastically. So, when they had said good-bye to their friends and families in Florence, the two young men set out on the long and dusty road to Rome.

II

THEY TRAVELED FOR MANY DAYS AND MANY NIGHTS across the hills and valleys, villages and farmlands. They passed shepherds who were leading their bleating flocks to pasture. They passed well-dressed merchants heading for faraway cities and bands of soldiers setting off to protect the interests of some wealthy lord or merchant. And sometimes the roads were empty for miles at a stretch; it was at times like this that they went cautiously, in fear of robbers who might be lying in wait for unprotected travelers.

But at last, they stood in safety at the top of a hill and looked about to the hills and valleys that held the remains of the once mighty city of Rome. As the sun nestled down behind the hills and turned the crumbling monuments a vivid shade of golden orange, Filippo felt sure that the knowledge he sought was here and that now his studies had begun.

The city of Rome had once been the center of the Roman Empire, which had ruled much of the known world. Roman architects and engineers of that time were unequaled, and the city had been a marvel of size and magnificence. There were amphitheaters built to seat the huge crowds who came

to watch the circuses and spectacles. There were temples to the many gods and goddesses the Romans worshipped, and there were luxurious baths—more like swimming pools to us—where the people met for health, sociability and rest. There were triumphal arches—tremendous gates built to commemorate the return of victorious generals and decorated with carvings of their conquests. And there were forums—collections of splendid buildings for business, politics and markets, where the citizens gathered every day. Surrounding all of these various public buildings were tall tenements of wood and brick where the common people lived. There were also comfortable private homes for the well-to-do that were equipped with such luxuries as central heating. And in and out of the city, leading to and coming from many distant lands, were the remarkable Roman roads.

Everything about Rome was over life-size; strength and power and shrewd, practical intelligence were the hallmarks of Roman civilization. But for many complex reasons the city was gradually weakened from within, and in 410 A.D. the first of many attacks on Rome by northern barbarian tribes began. People were kidnapped and killed, monuments were demolished and burned, and the golden coins and treasures of the city were stolen away. For hundreds of years Rome was repeatedly invaded and sacked by different peoples: first the barbarian northerners and later, in the ninth century, by the civilized and sophisticated Saracens, who were eager to conquer all of Europe. But only one year after a tremendous Saracen raid had taken place, an earthquake struck the city. It so ravaged Rome's remaining glories that there was little left to sack, and peace came at last.

Throughout the decline and many sackings of Rome the Popes of the Church remained in the city, trying to protect and save it, but they were powerless against such armies. At last, in 1309

the papal court moved to Avignon, in southern France. Here it remained for nearly seventy years, and Rome was then called "The Widowed City."

Finally, in 1378, the Pope was persuaded by St. Catherine of Siena to return to Rome. But his return to Italy was not accepted by many rulers, and so rival popes were set up in other cities, each claiming that he was the real Pope. Therefore, there was almost no worldly strength behind the Roman Pope until 1417, when it was at last established that Rome, and only Rome, could claim to be the home of the Popes.

It was sometime shortly before 1417, possibly just after 1401, we do not know exactly when, that Filippo and Donatello first arrived in Rome.

The place they found was very different from the modern, prosperous city of Florence they had left. In contrast to the palaces, markets and busy workshops of Florence they found mostly squalor and poverty and desolation. Many of the once busy streets of Rome were now little more than country cow paths. Among the massive arched skeletons of crumbling buildings, tall trees, sharp grass and prickly thistles grew. Under some of the moss-covered arches that were still intact, whole families had settled, making do with a bleak and leaking home as best they could. Swineherds brought their pigs to root among the broken columns, and the enormous reclining statues of calm, bearded river gods gazed mockingly at them. The lovely marble, decorated with carvings of cupids and emperors, gods and heroes, which covered the well-made brick walls, was being burnt into lime by the neighboring peasants to sweeten the earth of their fields.

But to Filippo these ruins held many secrets. Stripped bare as they were, exposing their inner construction devices, Filippo was able to see many things that would otherwise have remained hidden. He studied the thick walls and noted the solid rubble concrete filling them. He saw how this concrete was poured between two walls of timber and brick, which were held fast to one another with great iron clamps. He studied carefully the ingenious jigsaw puzzle grooves and protuberances carved at the joints that made one heavy stone grip and interlock with another. In the places where a building held the most weight, he found many ways used to hold and reinforce the walls, so that they did not collapse from the heavy masonry resting upon them. He made notes of the fact that the Romans had laid long plates of flat, hard stone over brick and rubble to bear a great load, and he made notes of the many ways arches were hidden in the walls, behind the marble facings, to strengthen them.

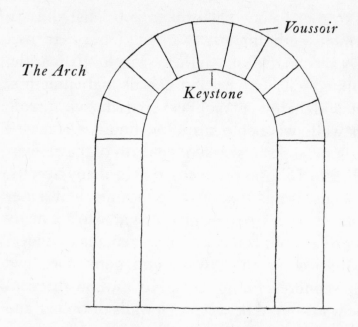

The Arch

Voussoir

Keystone

Again and again he observed the multiple uses of the arch—that remarkable structure that the Romans had learned from the ancient Etruscans and then put to their own uses. Although arches looked different and sometimes served different purposes, their construction was always basically the same.

Stones or bricks called voussoirs were cut in a wedge shape so that when they rested upon one another spanning an opening, their weight was thrust downward onto the one below, until finally the weight rested upon the walls from which the arch sprang. Since the voussoirs were cut wider at the top than at the bottom, they locked together when weight bore down upon them. The distance between walls or columns spanned by an arch made in this way could be greater than that spanned by a single horizontal unit such as a stone slab where the weight was distributed directly downward. An arch could be round or pointed, but it was the round arch that the Romans used most often. They had learned that if they built a ceiling with arches it was strong and also fireproof, because it was made of stone or brick rather than timber. For these reasons they had come to use arched, or as they are called, vaulted ceilings in their huge temples and other public buildings. If the arches were placed one after another in a horizontal row, they formed a vault shaped like a rounded tunnel. But if the arches sprang from the angles of a square and crossed one another, they formed a dome.

Although the principle of the arch was still used in Filippo's own time to construct smaller domes, the Roman system of vaulting over enormous spaces was not wholly understood. It was such vaulting that Filippo wanted to study. Most of the largest Roman domed temples had fallen down, but there remained one, miraculously intact, with a dome such as Filippo had seen only in his thoughts and never in actual masonry. This was the Pantheon, former temple of ancient gods and goddesses and now a Christian church. The dome had a diameter of over 140 feet, and it rose to more than that height above the ground. At the top it was lit by one huge round eye, thirty feet across, which was open to the sky.

Filippo spent many hours inside the Pantheon, watching the clouds that passed across the round eye and the long shafts of sunlight that fell to the marble floor. The light inside changed constantly as sunlight and shadows played upon the yellow marble of the dome. The space was vast and calm; it was like being inside a great, golden egg, enclosed and sheltered by it. Over and over, Filippo pondered the gentle swell of the tremendous arches, trying to understand the laws that had built and held them up for fifteen hundred years.

Months passed as Filippo and Donatello

The Pantheon

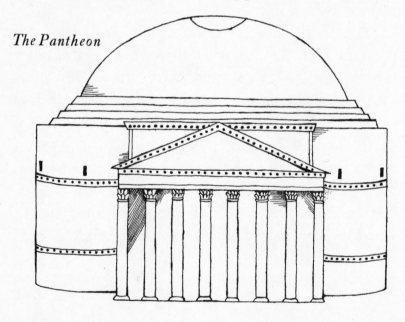

worked ceaselessly. When they discovered a statue or part of a building partially buried, they hired workmen to help them dig it up, in order to study it. People, seeing them, whispered that they were surely treasure seekers, who hoped to find a fortune in buried gold and jewels. And indeed, they did once find a small pot of coins that some Roman gentleman had buried for safekeeping long before.

After a time, however, although they had been as thrifty as possible, all of the money from the sale of Filippo's farm was gone. In Florence important commissions waited, so Donatello decided to return home and go back to work. But for Filippo it was too soon. The secrets of the Roman vaults and walls were only beginning to reveal themselves to him; his study of Rome was not yet complete. He decided to remain and do some work as a goldsmith, which would earn him the money he needed to stay.

It probably was not easy for Filippo to say good-bye to Donatello, for there would be no one left to talk of home or of the work he loved. But learning about the buildings of Rome meant more to him than anything, and he was willing to give up many other things in order to live with them for a little longer.

As for Donatello, he would never be the same again. Antique sculpture had taught him that long before men had made marble or bronze seem alive, and that the most fleeting expression or gesture could be held forever in the hardest of materials. The heroes and gods and cupids that had adorned ancient Rome could be transformed in his statues into something new and fresh and beautiful. The human body, he saw, could be the measure of many things; all thoughts and feeling, it seemed, could be portrayed through its image. The possibilities were more than enough to keep him busy for the rest of his life.

After Donatello had gone, Filippo began to work harder than ever. He learned, after much observation, to recognize the three classical orders of architecture, which the Romans had inherited from the first great European city-builders, the Greeks. These orders were identified by the three kinds of stone columns that held up the roofs of buildings. There were specific rules for their use.

The first and oldest order was the Doric. It was said that the proper proportion for a Doric column was a height six times its thickness at the base of the shaft, because a man's foot was equal to one-sixth of his height. The column was usually fluted. The capital at the head of the column was plain and unadorned. In these ways the column showed the muscular strength and stability of a strong, athletic man.

Next came the Ionic. The ancient builders here wished for a column with a slimmer, more graceful look, so they decided that the proportions of a woman should be used. Therefore, the Ionic specifications called for a column eight times as tall as its thickness at the base of the shaft. Upon the capital were coils of stone on either side called volutes. These represented the curly ringlets that Greek women wore. Beneath ran a row of carving representing festoons of flowers and fruit worn in the hair. Down the entire shaft ran flutes, which were the heavy folds of a woman's robe.

Last of all came the Corinthian. It was said, in legend, that the death of a lovely girl had inspired this order. She had lived in ancient Greece, and after she took sick and died, her unhappy nurse had collected some of her best loved possessions in a tall, slender basket and left them upon her tomb. The nurse covered the basket with a roof tile to protect the contents from the wind and rain. It was winter when the basket was put on the grave; and the nurse could not see that an acanthus plant usually grew in that place. When spring came the acanthus pushed up out of the earth and grew up along the sides of the basket. It grew and grew, until it reached the large roof tile. Since it now could grow no taller, it bent its leaves and curled downwards. When a famous architect walked by and saw the basket sitting on the young girl's tomb, with the tender green leaves growing around it, he was delighted with the sweet delicacy of the form, and drew a picture of it. Soon after, he was called to the city of Corinth to build a temple. He decided to invent a new and elegant style of column, using the down-curling acanthus leaves for the capital, and the tall and slender proportions of a young girl for the shaft. The Corinthians were greatly pleased with this design, and it became the third order.

Where Filippo found temples still intact, he studied the roofs that these different orders of columns supported, and learned to recognize their parts. The roofs of such buildings were generally pitched: two flat areas slanting from the center toward the ground, forming a triangular area between the roof and the columns at the ends of the building. This triangular area is called the pediment, and the horizontal area between the columns and the pediment is called the entablature. This entablature is made up of three sections: architrave, frieze and cornice; the relationship of all these parts to one another was largely determined by the style of column supporting them. Filippo learned from extensive observation and measurement to distinguish the fitting proportion for each

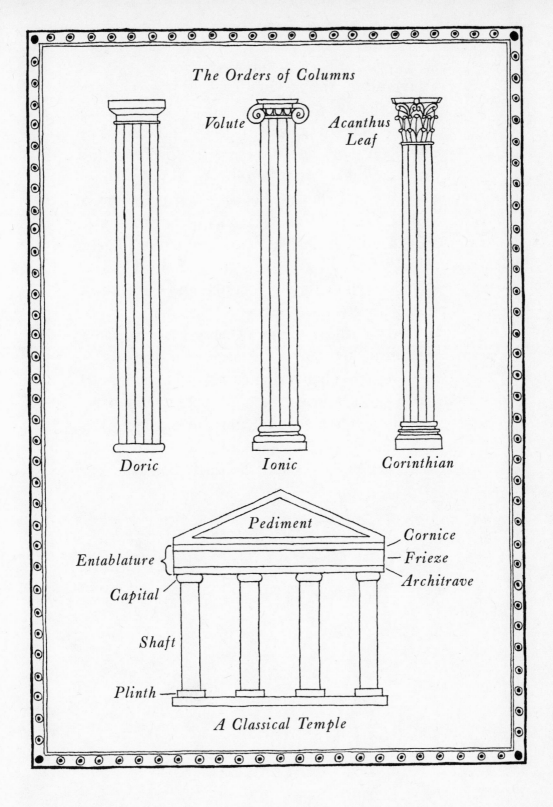

The Orders of Columns

Doric

Volute

Ionic

Acanthus Leaf

Corinthian

Pediment

Entablature

Capital

Shaft

Plinth

Cornice

Frieze

Architrave

A Classical Temple

style. All along the foundations and ruins of ancient temples he walked, measuring and making mysterious notes to himself, measuring the distance between columns, the total length of the colonnade or row of columns, and the relationship of the sections of the entablature. He also saw decorations carved on fallen marble sections of cornices and friezes that were new and lovely to him. There were realistically carved festoons of flowers and fruit, the overflowing cornucopia, and the scallop shell in its perfect symmetry.

Every day these things became more familiar to him until they seemed to become a part of his own thoughts. What had once been the mammoth Baths of Diocletian was now a series of vine-covered, tumbledown vaults towering above the ruined city. When Filippo climbed to the top of the fallen vaults to look at the inner construction

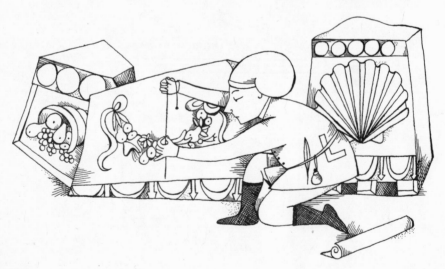

of the arches, he would stop to rest, and look at the fallen monuments below. Gradually he came to see them, not as dilapidated ruins, but complete and perfect as they once had been. He became able to visualize some of the ways he thought these giant buildings had been constructed, and it was at times like this that he was happiest.

As he gazed at Rome, a new picture formed in his mind; he saw a new Florence, more magnificent than the old. It was as though Rome were born again, looking as Filippo imagined she once had. He re-invented new temples, new palaces, and then he crowned his city with a lovely dome. He had been in Rome now for more than two years, and he had solved most of the architectural problems that had baffled him. A little more time, and he believed he would be ready to go home and begin to build.

It was just at this point that Filippo became ill. He developed a high fever, which passed, but his strength did not return as it should have. In Florence there were skilled doctors and apothecaries, but not in Rome, and so Filippo decided to go home and let them make him well again.

Reluctantly, he said good-bye to his beloved ruins and carefully packed all of his drawings and measurements. Then he set out, tired and ill, for his home in Florence that he had not seen for so long.

III

AFTER RETURNING TO FLORENCE, FILIPPO RAPIDLY recovered. He enthusiastically spoke to everyone he knew of all that he had seen and learned in Rome. Many citizens were excited over his drawings of Roman architecture and asked him to re-model buildings for them in the antique style. As time passed he was called upon more frequently as an architect than as a sculptor-goldsmith, and he was well known and admired for his building skills.

To say, however, that his buildings were in the antique style of Rome is not true. For Filippo had a mind so original that he could not possibly have slavishly imitated a style that had gone before. Instead, he had studied and absorbed the forms and motifs of Roman architecture so thoroughly that his own ideas were permanently shaped by them. But the ways in which he used his knowledge of Roman architecture were always his own. His buildings are like nothing that had come before; they were in a new style and one that was rapidly recognized by Filippo's contemporaries as being especially fitting for the new age that had come into being.

For it was a new age; today we know it as the Italian Renaissance. In Florence, new ideas were

constantly being born and welcomed as a delight and a challenge. Men sought and found knowledge with gaiety and enthusiasm. They looked, as Filippo had, to the past as a guide, and then they looked, with clear mental eyes, at the world around them, and shaped new thoughts.

One such man was a philosopher and mathematician named Paolo Toscanelli. He met Filippo and, impressed by his quick intelligence and eagerness to learn, offered to teach him the mysterious sciences of geometry and other mathematical systems. Filippo was overjoyed at this opportunity and joined Toscanelli's other pupil-friends, when they met.

Daring ideas were discussed in this group: ideas not only on mathematics but on astronomy and cosmography, which were the sciences of the heavens and the earth. Just as Filippo thought about shaping space in his buildings, these men thought about what shape the earth and surrounding universe *really* were. Some years later another disciple of Toscanelli's wondered with him whether the earth was really flat, as was then thought, or round, as they were convinced it was. This man was Christopher Columbus. When, in his eagerness to prove that the world was round, he sailed west for the Indies, it was a map drawn by Toscanelli that guided him.

In Filippo's time, mathematics was not the practical system that we know today. Many of its ideas were unproved, and it was primarily theoretical and philosophical. Filippo, however, discovered many practical uses for his new knowledge of mathematics. He, for one thing, worked out a system to make his drawings represent space more accurately. This was a geometric system whereby he established a fixed point on the far horizon line and then proceeded to have all of the points that began in the foreground meet and cross at this vanishing point. In this way, he could accurately establish the relative sizes of things as they receded into the distance and thereby give a great illusion of reality. This system, called linear perspective, helped Filippo greatly in drawing both existing buildings and imaginary ones that he hoped to build. Infinite and complex were the problems that he set up and worked out in perspective.

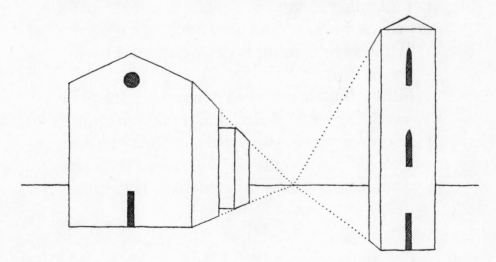

He had two friends who were painters, named Tommaso Masaccio and Paolo Uccello. When they saw Filippo's perspective studies they were eager to learn how to do it. As painters, they were interested in learning how to create a real-seeming space on a flat surface. They wanted their paintings to seem more like worlds in themselves, where real figures moved back and forth in a real space. Filippo taught them all he had discovered about perspective, and his eager pupils immediately began to use the system in their commissions. Perspective became the fashion in Florentine workshops, and no painter thereafter could call himself fit to earn a living without some knowledge of it.

Paolo Uccello became so entranced with working out perspective problems that he neglected all else. He forgot to eat; he forgot to sleep; and he forgot to finish important commissions. His wife and friends would remind him that there were, after all, other things in life, but it is said that he only shook his head and answered:

"How sweet a thing is this perspective!"

Filippo built many buildings and at some point was asked to give his opinion regarding the future of the cathedral. He suggested that, first of all, an octagonal drum should be built above the crossing, from which the dome could eventually spring.

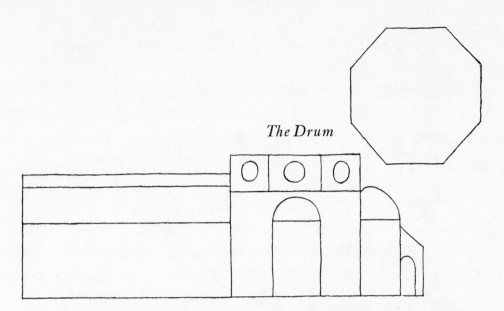

The Drum

By this device, the dome would not have too heavy and low a look. Work on the drum proceeded accordingly, but the dome remained to be built and years passed by. But one day, in 1418, a public proclamation was made. It said that if anyone wished to submit plans or models suggesting a design for the dome, they would be viewed and considered by the Board of Works. If any ideas seemed worth considering, the artists who had submitted them would be further commissioned to make a more extensive plan.

As had happened seventeen years before, the competition quickly fell between two men—Filippo and his old rival, Lorenzo Ghiberti. The Board of Works suggested that each of them build a large model for further consideration.

Although Filippo had recognized his inferiority to Ghiberti in the matter of the Baptistery doors, he did not believe that Ghiberti, who had no knowledge of architecture, was in any way equal in this matter of the dome. For many, many years Filippo had dreamed of this opportunity, and he had at last thought of a way by which the enormous dome could be built.

He began, in secret, to build a large model of the dome. In this he was helped by his old and loyal friend Donatello and another artist named Nanni d'Antonio di Banchi. This man was an uninspired artist, but an excellent craftsman, particularly in

carpentry, and therefore helpful. Together the three of them began the arduous task of constructing a wood and brick model of Filippo's plan. No one was allowed to see this model in progress, however, for the competition between artists was so great that Filippo was certain that his daring idea would be stolen from him.

Although Filippo was working on his model, Ghiberti seemed not to be especially interested. He continued his work on the still unfinished doors of the Baptistery. The Board of Works and the Guild of the Art of Wool then decided that the contest should include models and plans from architects from all over Europe. In this way, they reasoned, all ideas could be seen and discussed and the genius of the best builders available could be used, if they chose. Some say that Filippo himself made this suggestion, in order to demonstrate his knowledge not only to Florence but to the world! And perhaps it was so. In any case, to all Florentine merchants and ambassadors living abroad, the following message was sent:

> *Spare no expense nor trouble to invite the best master builders to Florence, that they may enter the competition to build the dome of St. Mary of the Flower.*

But, when this message went out, Filippo had decided to return to Rome. He felt the need to refresh his thoughts with the sight of Rome; furthermore, he believed that if he were away, his reputation would be enhanced. People would talk about him, compare him with others, and ask him to return home. For while he believed that he was the one man in the world able to build the dome, he also believed that a good deal of ingenuity was going to be required to convince the Board of Works that he was the right, and only, man.

And so, once again, he departed for Rome.

As he left Florence, the other master builders began to arrive.

From across the Alps they came; from across the Mediterranean Sea to Genoa and Pisa they came. The cathedral-builders of the green and fertile land of France came, and the men who built the great town halls of the Low Countries came. From dry and desert Spain they came—the builders of cool, lacy gardens in stone, and the men who had raised the many-spired universities against the misty sky of England came. And from Germany they came—the land of evergreen forests and tall and sober churches. With plans, drawings, and models they came—each one hoping that he could raise the dome.

Meanwhile, in Rome, Filippo wandered among

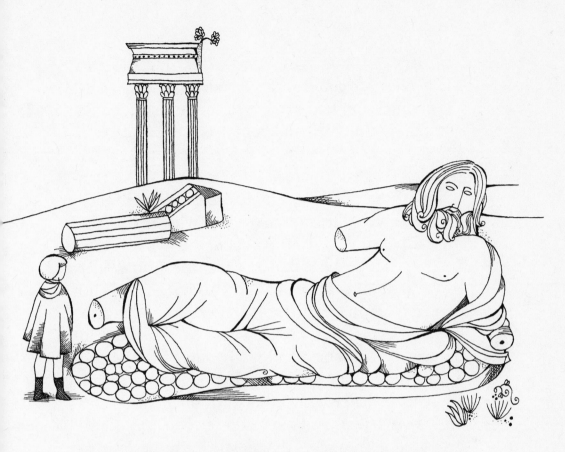

the familiar ruins, waiting for the messenger who,
he was certain, would come and invite him to return home and enter his name among the compet-
ing masters.

At last the long-awaited messenger arrived, and
Filippo rode back with him to Florence.

IV

As they entered the city gates, Filippo and the messenger could sense the air of festivity that the competition had given to Florence. Pride and anticipation seemed to shout from every corner, for the erection of the dome represented to the people of the city a victory over the impossible and a sign of their civic virtue and strength. And then too, there were the foreign masters who were arriving daily with their assistants and servants from faraway lands. The likes of them the Florentines had seldom, if ever, seen. There were bearded and befurred Germans; French masters from the Burgundian courts wearing elaborate headdresses and opulent velvet robes; and many other strange and exotic foreigners, speaking in tongues that few Florentines had ever heard. All of the public lodgings were taken, and even the farmers and shepherds made frequent trips down from the hills to see and hear the fascinating strangers. No one talked about anything but the competion, and many wild guesses were made as to what the outcome would be. What would the dome look like—who would be the master chosen to construct it? For no one doubted that the contest would bring results and that the cathedral would, after so many years, be crowned with a proud and glorious dome.

One man, however, paid little attention to the excitement. This was Filippo. He kept to himself, busy at work on the construction of his model of the dome, which although miniature must be perfect in every way.

When, at last, all of the invited masters had arrived, a great assembly was held. Here, with much ceremony, the competition officially began. Before the magistrates of Florence and the Board of Works, each master rose in turn to speak at length on his proposed means of raising the dome and to demonstrate plans and models.

One of the greatest obstacles was the fact that the building of any dome had always required a structure made of heavy timber built up from the ground to support the heavy stones until all were in place. When the dome was completed, the wooden support, or centering as it was called, was removed and the arches supported themselves. It had long been obvious, however, to anyone who had thought about the problem, that for this dome, centering was out of the question. The diameter of the crossing was 135 feet, and the walls of the cathedral were 140 feet high. Above the walls of the crossing was the drum, constructed to hold the dome; this drum was thirty feet high, meaning that the walls from which the dome would begin to spring were already 170 feet high. In all history, no dome had ever been placed upon walls this high. The quantity of timber that would be required to erect a centering within this area was prohibitive in cost. Therefore, a major problem was really how to devise a new way of supporting the heavy stones during construction.

Many and varied suggestions were offered by the foreign masters. One master believed that if a huge mound of earth and coins was piled high within the walls, the dome could be supported during construction by this. Later, when the mighty arches spanned the walls, the mound could be removed by the citizens, who would carry away many pails of earth in the hope of finding riches there! Another suggested that the dome be built of light and airy volcanic pumice stone to lessen its weight. Others insisted that a permanent column must be built in the center of the crossing for the arches to rest upon.

As the magistrates listened to all of the strange plans that were offered, they began to think that perhaps the competition had been in vain. Of all these master builders, not one really seemed able to successfully raise the dome.

Much time went by, and at last the day came when all the guests had spoken and the local masters could have their say. Each spoke in turn, and each outlined the difficulties that everyone already knew. At last it was Filippo's turn.

He rose before the grand assembly—a small, bald, and insignificant-looking man. Before him stood no model, no plans—nothing at all. He began to speak, as the others had, of the many difficulties they faced. Then he mentioned difficulties no one else had even thought of. It sounded as though he was telling them that constructing the dome was not possible. But, after he had finished outlining all of the problems, he suddenly proceeded to say:

"But gentlemen . . . I believe that nothing is truly impossible. I can raise the dome. I can raise it without mounds of earth . . . without the use of pumice stone . . . without a column in the center. In fact, I can raise it with no supporting frame at all."

Then he sat down, and after a minute of surprised silence, everyone began to laugh. What he said seemed ridiculous, and the magistrates did not try to hide their scorn when they asked him to show them his model in order to prove his ability to perform such a miracle.

Filippo answered that he would not show his model in public, for fear that his revolutionary idea would be stolen from him. But loudly he insisted that he alone could, and would, build the dome. He tried to explain his plan to them, but no one understood him. The more he explained, the more he was laughed at, and the more he was laughed at, the more angry he became until at last he shouted in frustration and fury at the city magistrates and the learned masters.

At this outburst, he was ordered to leave. He refused, so the guards were called and he was put out bodily, into the street. When he had gone, everyone said that he was obviously a poor fool who had lost his mind, that he had no business upsetting the dignity of such a grand occasion.

And so, humiliated and ashamed, Filippo went home. The day that he had worked and waited for had come, and gone. He had nothing to show for his years and years of effort except the name of "Filippo the Fool."

V

FILIPPO WAS FILLED WITH DESPAIR. HE KEPT TO his house for fear he had become the laughing-stock of all Florence. Many times he came close to destroying his meticulously constructed model and all of the careful studies that had gone into it. But his friends Donatello and Luca della Robbia came to visit him often and soothed his hurt feelings. They reported any gossip that they had heard regarding the competition, and they reminded him that the magistrates were often fickle and inconsistent. With the kind help of his friends, Filippo recovered his courage and made up his mind to try again.

Now he began to attempt, by subtle persuasion, to regain the opportunity that temper had lost for him. He took aside various influential members of the committee and quietly, patiently tried again to explain his theory. As the assembly dragged on with less and less chance of success, the magistrates were more willing to listen, though they still did not understand. Finally they pleaded with Filippo to re-enter the competition and to forgive them for dismissing him so rudely. Filippo agreed to do so. It was decided that whoever could make an egg stand upright should be the winner—and architect for the construction of the dome.

So all of the learned masters proceeded to make complicated structures to support a rolling egg. The day came for judging the entries, and all of the masters arrived. But as each one demonstrated his structure, his egg began to roll. Sometimes it rolled just a little from side to side—and sometimes it rolled right off the table, onto the floor.

Once more Filippo took his turn. Once more he had no model, no construction, no drawings, nothing but one little egg. Quickly and with precision he tapped the egg on the surface of the table, flattened one end, and the egg stood—alone—unsupported—upright!

"Ahhhhhh . . ." cried the learned masters, when they saw this. "Any of us could have done *that*!"

"And so could any of you have built the dome, had you seen my model," replied Filippo.

And in this way, the contest was won by Filippo.

The learned masters returned to their homes, certain that the Florentines were not the shrewd men that they were said to be, but dreamers and

madmen, like the crazy architect they had chosen to build the dome.

Filippo then revealed his model to the judges. He also read a paper he had written, which eloquently explained his proposed means of erecting the dome.

He had decided that it was impossible to build a single dome by means of semicircular arches, like the Pantheon and other Roman domes, because the tremendous downward and outward thrust of the weight of the voussoirs would cause the walls to burst apart and collapse. A pointed arch, however, did not exert as strong an outward thrust and required less thick walls to rest upon than a round arch did. Therefore, he decided to build the dome with a pointed arch and to have two domes, one over the other. The outer dome would act as a protective shell for the heavier inner one and would also give to the dome a fuller, more swelling silhouette. The two domes would be constructed at the same time and clamped together by various means as they were built. At the angles of

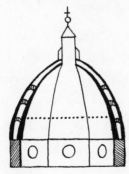

Cross Section of Dome

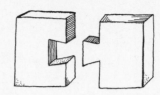

the octagon from which the arches would spring, the heavy stones were to be dovetailed together. (Dovetailing is a technique for firmly joining two sections of wood or stone. Into one section a slanted groove is cut. The section to be joined with it is cut to produce a slanted protuberance that exactly fits the groove. The second section is slid into the first from the side. When the two are united, they cannot be pulled apart for the inside section of the protruding piece is wider than the opening of the groove through which it would have to pass.) In other places the stones were to be clamped together with timber and iron braces. In yet other places the two domes themselves would be held together by small supporting arches of masonry and timber. Every device for securing stones to one another that Filippo had discovered in his Roman studies was a help to him now. He made use of many of the old devices that he had seen, and invented many new ones of his own.

These means of fastening stones together would all help Filippo overcome the problem of centering. He planned to build the dome in rings of concentric circular vaulting. Two things would

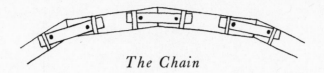

prevent this vaulting from collapsing before the arch action was sufficiently strong to hold it up. One would be the absolute security and rigidity of the voussoirs that formed the vaults. This would be accomplished by assuring a tight fit of each stone to another. Then timber and iron chains would gird the outer circumference of the inner dome wherever the downward and outward thrust of the arch action was strongest. This chainwork would relieve the lower walls of the cathedral of much of their burden of supporting the mammoth dome. It would also keep the vault rigid and prevent its bursting apart at points of great stress.

The dome was to be built in this manner to a height of about 116 feet above the octagonal drum. At the top of the dome, the inner and outer vaults would meet and join. A circular eye at the center would light the interior, and this eye was to be protected from the elements by a small, circular, roofed building set upon the dome. This was called the lantern. When they were loaded with the lantern, the arches would be further stabilized.

The lower sections of the vaults were to be built of hard stone, and the upper sections were to be built of brick or some other lightweight stone. The vaults would lessen in thickness as they grew higher. This was to make the dome as light in weight as possible, thus reducing somewhat the pressure on the lower walls. In the space between the two vaults, a staircase would be built so that the dome could be climbed.

This, then, was the essence of Filippo's daring plan. It is no wonder that no one understood him when he first spoke of it, for any method of constructing a dome without centering was then unknown. Furthermore, no such method had been known even to the Roman builders. The plan was original and without precedent and no one really knew whether or not it would work. But Filippo had obviously given much thought to this plan; no detail had been overlooked, and his thoroughness and self-confidence impressed many skeptics.

Unfortunately, not all of the judges on the competition committee were entirely convinced that it was possible. They began to dispute among

themselves. Because no one could fully understand Filippo's idea, those who believed he could do it were acting on faith—faith in only one man. But there were others who doubted Filippo's ability, and said:

"Why should one man, who is perhaps wrong, be given such great responsibility, when our city has so many gifted men?"

The arguments continued and grew more fierce. Throughout the city, the issue was debated. Should Filippo Brunelleschi be given, all alone, such an awesome responsibility on mere faith? Should he not perhaps have a partner in his work who might help him to keep his feet on the ground and his head out of the clouds?

At last, in order to silence the arguments and get on with the work, the committee decided that the voice of the people must be listened to. For this reason they decided to appoint a co-worker for Filippo who would share with him half the title and salary that had been set aside for the architect of the dome. The man they chose was Lorenzo Ghiberti.

Why Ghiberti? He had no experience as an architect, although his skill in sculpture was unsurpassed by anyone but Donatello. He had contributed no ideas worth considering to the problem of construction—indeed, he had not really seemed terribly interested in it other than for the glory it might bring to his already famous name. The choice seems to have been a purely political one. Ghiberti, although genuinely gifted in his work, was also greedy, conceited and ambitious. He had learned while young to flatter the right people and consequently had many friends in powerful positions. For this reason, the old rivalry between Filippo and Ghiberti arose again more bitter than ever before.

Privately, Filippo was furious. To Donatello he raged on about the peculiar quality of the Florentines that made each man among them think he knew more about everything than the most experienced experts. Filippo was right; they were this way, but they were something more, too.

Intelligent, free-thinking, in awe of no one, the Florentines took a fierce and passionate interest in the way their city looked. No people since the Athenian Greeks of the fifth century B.C. had been so concerned with beauty in their city and so convinced that it was as necessary to life as food and drink. If at times, their interest exceeded its proper limits, it was only because their pursuit of excellence was so intense. From their artists they demanded, and usually received, only the best. Donatello told Filippo of how, when he had spent some time in the neighboring city of Padua making a statue, everyone praised everything he did. At first Donatello was delighted, accustomed as he was to the never-satisfied Florentines. But after a while, the endless praise began to worry him and he hurried home to Florence as soon as he could, out of fear that he would grow self-satisfied and mediocre under such a constant diet of praise.

Filippo was aware that there was some truth in this. So because he was certain that he could prove himself worthy of building the dome alone, he decided to be tactful and patient and wait for the right opportunity to rid himself of Ghiberti. Publicly, he appeared to accept willingly this indignity rather than risk losing the fulfillment of all his hopes.

Preparation for the work began. Eight master builders and their accompanying crews of masons were hired; stones and timber were assembled; framework and scaffolding for the masons were built; and on the 7th of August, 1420, construction began. On this day the city voted to spend sufficient money to buy a cask of the finest red wine, white bread and the best fresh melons so that Filippo, Ghiberti and the eight master builders could hold a little party to celebrate the occasion.

Nearly twenty years had passed since Filippo had first begun to think about it; and now, at last, he was going to build his dome.

VI

As Filippo had expected, Ghiberti made no interference, but kept to his own work. He continued, however, to draw half the salary as co-architect of the dome. Filippo said nothing of this and worked hard.

Not a brick was fired, not a stone was carved that Filippo did not carefully examine to make certain that it was perfect. When the stones for the voussoirs were quarried out of the earth, Filippo was there, watching to make certain that only the best stone was taken. When, as sometimes inevitably happened, a piece of stone had a fault or hole, Filippo would cut a turnip and plug the hole to make an absolutely accurate guide for the masons to follow when they repaired it. Not a workman arrived in the early dawn who did not find Filippo there before him, and when the sun set in the hills, Filippo was the last to leave.

At first much time was wasted as the masons climbed up and down the height of the walls to the scaffolding where they worked, and so Filippo designed a scaffolding that accommodated cooks and wineshops so that the workmen did not need to come down during the day, once they were settled. His old love of mechanics and clock-making enabled him to invent and construct machines to

transport mammoth stones safely up past the walls, through the air, to the high scaffolding where the workmen stood.

Though his was a grand and noble vision, Filippo did not forget small and practical details of architecture. He had little holes spaced throughout the dome, in order that the wind should not blow too hard against a solid mass, but could pass through, its force somewhat spent. He also remembered to attach hooks to the inside of the vault so that a scaffolding could later be hung, in case murals should ever be painted upon the interior surface. He remembered to place rain spouts of marble wherever needed so that the rain could run off the dome efficiently. Some of his admirers compared him with Daedalus, the master inventor-architect of Greek mythology, and even said that Daedalus had been born again in Filippo. It was difficult, even for those who were skeptical of his ideas, not to admit that they appeared to work better than anyone had anticipated.

And as he built, Filippo's confidence grew. Two years passed, and all the work went well. Ghiberti continued to do nothing, and Filippo grew more determined than ever to be rid of him.

The vaults were nearly twelve feet high and the time had come to bind the inner vault with the great iron and timber chain. Upon the success of this chain, the success of the whole construction rested. Consequently, Filippo had worked out the design for it most carefully.

Then one day, shortly before the chain was to be built, Filippo did not arrive at the cathedral square at his usual time. The masons, accustomed to receiving precise instructions from him every morning, were unable to proceed with their work and idled in front of the cathedral. Filippo did not come all day.

Later, a delegation of important citizens called on Filippo at his home. They found him in bed, with his head wrapped in a towel. He seemed very, very sick. He began to talk feebly and pathetically of what might happen to the dome if he were to die. Could Ghiberti take charge of the work alone? No one knew, and Filippo suggested that perhaps Lorenzo should make the chain and prove, by this act, his competence.

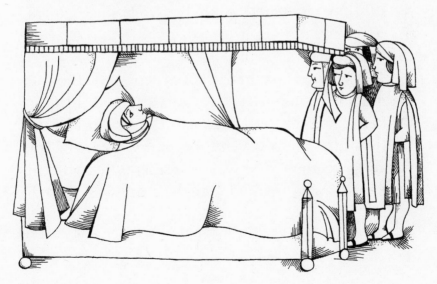

Ghiberti agreed to make a model of the chain, confident that he could, for he was an excellent craftsman.

All work stopped while Ghiberti worked on his model for the chain. Filippo lay low, eagerly awaiting its completion, and all the while pretending to be sick in bed.

At last Ghiberti completed his chain. But when he demonstrated it before the magistrates, it was clear, even to them, that it was not strong enough and would never hold. Filippo then asked how Ghiberti could be expected to take over the work, should it be necessary, when he was obviously incompetent to do so. At this the magistrates realized that Filippo had no intention of recovering from his illness until Ghiberti was relieved of his title. They then let it be known, somewhat to Ghiberti's disgrace, that Filippo was the sole architect and overseer for the construction of the dome.

Filippo recovered from his pretended illness immediately and went to work more enthusiastically than ever before.

The seasons changed, the years passed, and the great dome rounded upward. But after Filippo got the better of Ghiberti, his enemies began to speak badly of him again. Even though the results of his building seemed to speak for themselves, there were many who insisted that the dome would collapse before it was finished. One year there were a large number of particularly bad thunderstorms. Whenever the thunder and lightning flashed in the sky behind the great dome, people said that Filippo was inviting the envy and anger of Heaven itself, in daring to build so high. Surely, they said, no good would come of it.

One of the leaders of Filippo's opposition was a public reader of the works of Dante. He wrote some satirical poems that made fun of Filippo and his ambitious undertaking. These poems were circulated throughout the city. Unfortunately, although he had read Dante's beautiful rhythms over and over, he had absorbed little from them, and his own poems were clumsy and poorly written. Filippo could not resist the opportunity to compose some verses of his own, in answer to these, making as much fun of the poet's lack of skill as the poet had made fun of him. Filippo too was a student of Dante, and in poetry, as in architecture, his sure sense of grace, precision and rhythm showed. He composed some elegant and witty verses that put the public reader quite to shame.

One year some of Filippo's enemies began to talk to the workmen about the dangerous work that they were doing. And it was dangerous. Two men had fallen to their deaths in the ten years that

construction had been going on. The masons willing to work at such heights were brave, and even occasionally reckless men. At one time, Filippo had discovered some workmen, secured only by a rope, sliding down the great outer curve of the dome, for sport! They enjoyed stealing baby birds and eggs from the nests that swallows and pigeons built upon the dome. A law was quickly passed, making it a serious offense to steal baby birds or eggs from the cathedral dome, and this stopped. But now discontent spread among the workmen. As the dome curved inward without any visible support, the work grew more and more awesome and frightening. The men reasoned that they should be paid more for such dangerous work and went on strike for higher wages.

Actually, the danger of the work had been considered in establishing the workmen's pay, and Filippo saw the strike as unreasonable. Feeling certain it was the work of his enemies, he determined to fight as best he could. He quickly left Florence and went north to Lombardy, where he hired a group of Lombard masons. Returning with them promptly to Florence, he instructed them in his methods, and with scarcely any delay, work continued.

The Florentine masons were chagrined to discover that they could be so easily replaced. They begged Filippo to reinstate them, which he did.

The dome continued to grow and curve inward, as if by magic. Filippo devised a scaffolding that hid the sight of the void below. In this way the workmen would not grow dizzy and perhaps fall.

By 1432 the dome was nearly at its intended height of 116 feet above the octagon. The total height from the ground was nearly 295 feet. Nothing like it had ever before been seen. The Board of Works, seeing that it was so nearly complete, instructed Filippo to submit a model for the lantern in order that they might decide on its design.

But by 1434, when the dome rounded over the great central space of the crossing, the magistrates had decided that the church itself needed some renovation before the ceremony of consecration could take place. And they had decided to consecrate the cathedral before the lantern was placed upon the dome's summit. This would allow them to take advantage of an unexpected opportunity. At the time, the Pope had fled from some enemies in Rome, and had been given sanctuary in Florence. In return for the hospitality of the Florentines, he had agreed to consecrate the cathedral himself.

All activity now went into the renovation and decoration of the church for the solemn ceremony. All of the craftsmen in Florence were engaged in making paintings, carpets, tapestries, vestments, altarpieces, candelabra, floral decorations, banners, and all of the other magnificent items required for the consecration ceremony. The Florentines loved pageantry, and this was the kind of opportunity for glorious display that did not

present itself often. So, while everyone else prepared for the consecration ceremony, Filippo
worked quietly and without fanfare on his model
for the lantern. The dome looked incomplete without it—it was to be the jewel for the crown. To
Filippo, it was very important.

On March 25th, 1436, Pope Eugene IV per-
formed the consecration ceremony. Now at last the
people had their cathedral. Furthermore, it was
crowned by a dome more magnificent than any the
world had ever seen.

Shortly after the consecration, another ceremony took place. On that day, the Board of Works
spent sufficient money to pay many trumpeters
and fifers, and to buy bread, wine, meat, fruit,
cheese and macaroni. All of this was given to
Filippo, the masters, the workmen and the priests
in order that they might hold for themselves a
grand party, celebrating the completion of their
glorious work.

VII

ONE CAN ONLY ASSUME THAT THE FLORENTINES loved competition for its own sake. For how else can one explain the fact that in the fall of 1436, shortly after the consecration ceremony had taken place, a public competition was held, open to any and all who wished to enter, a competition to choose the architect for the lantern of the dome! After Filippo's remarkable victory in erecting the dome—a feat called impossible by so many—it would seem as though he had earned the right to see it to completion. And yet, he was required to submit his model for the lantern, along with many others, to the Board of Works.

And there were many others! Everyone in Florence, it seemed, felt qualified to design the lantern. Since it did not require, in its design, the great technical skill of the dome, many amateurs felt that they were qualified to submit a design. The problem was primarily aesthetic. The dome required, for its proper effect, the lantern, and Filippo had always planned on building a lantern that was in perfect harmony with the dome.

The competition, however, was like a sporting event, and the citizens seem to have enjoyed themselves thoroughly. The entries were many, and most of them were bad. People were amused to dis-

74

cover that there was even a model that had been submitted by a lady, a most unheard of thing. And, in spite of his ignominious dismissal from the work, Lorenzo Ghiberti could not resist submitting his own design.

But one model stood out, for it was perfect in every way. This was Filippo's. The Board of Works wasted little time naming him the victor, and they wrote a revealing document explaining their choice.

They explained that a public competition had been held, open to any and all who wished to join. After fair and impartial judging of all the entries, the Board of Works had decided that Filippo Brunelleschi's model was the best for many reasons. It was the most waterproof; it admitted to the dome the maximum amount of light; it was the strongest and at the same time, the lightest in weight; its construction details were the best thought out; and most important of all, it was the most graceful and pleasing to look at. Therefore, the Board of Works had decided to name Filippo, and only Filippo, as architect of the lantern and all other matters relating to the dome, for the rest of his life, come what may. Furthermore, the document decreed, all citizens must accept this decision as final and irrevocable and cease all malevolent criticism and acts against Filippo and his staff.

Was this then the purpose of the seemingly silly competition? Was it so that Filippo could, for the first time, be free from the envy and rivalry that had been such a problem? Now, after sixteen years of work, he was given complete freedom to do as he wished regarding the dome.

Immediately after the decision was made, Filippo, accompanied by three master masons, went to visit the marble quarries at Campigli. Here he spent some time choosing and ordering the finest marble available.

Then, for reasons we do not know, work appears to have stopped. The city of Florence suffered at this time from many complex problems. Other things were given priority over the work on the dome, and there seems to have been a serious

shortage of funds available for its completion. In 1440, work on the lantern was still not begun; Filippo's salary and those of the master masons employed by him were cut by half.

Five more years went by until at last, in 1445, Filippo was directed to begin work on the lantern. All of the snowy marble was gathered in front of the cathedral, and the task of hauling the stones up to the top, nearly three hundred feet in the air, began.

But Filippo was never to see the lantern completed. In 1446, at the age of sixty-nine, he died and was buried in the cathedral. He was mourned by the entire city and most especially by the younger and poorer artists, whom he had always found time to help. His life had been his work. He had lived simply, he had never married, and he had had no separation of his work and his play. Both were one to him.

So perfect was his model for the lantern that the master builders he had employed were able to complete the design with no changes whatsoever. Today it sits, delicate, poised, and graceful, upon the summit of the massive dome. It is like a dainty little marble temple in the sky. It is composed of many of the classical Roman elements Filippo loved: the Corinthian column, the scallop shell, the round arch, and the curved spiral volute.

During his lifetime, Filippo had built many other buildings in Florence: palaces, churches, and the beautiful Foundling Hospital for the poor orphans of the city. All of his work is characterized by a delight in simple, harmonious, rational spaces. His buildings give pleasure through their precise and mathematical beauty. Many of the elements of classical architecture—particularly the Doric, Ionic and Corinthian columns and the pediment over a window—were used over and over again by Filippo in his buildings. These elements became as characteristic of the Italian Renaissance as they had been of Greek and Roman civilization. As he had dreamed of doing many years earlier in Rome, Filippo had transformed his city and had built for her new glories. Then he had crowned them with a dome.

The dome still stands, sturdy as when it was built, over 500 years ago. Its soaring curves are as restful and dignified as the outline of the hills, and at the same time, as fresh and surprising as the violets that cover the hills each spring. They say that its mighty shadow would shelter all of the people in Tuscany, were they to gather beneath it. When a Florentine is far from home and lonely, he has his own expression for homesickness. He says:

"I am sick for the sight of the Dome."

EPILOGUE

ABOUT A HUNDRED YEARS AFTER FILIPPO'S DEATH, another Florentine artist went to Rome. This artist, one of the most remarkable that Florence gave to the world, was Michelangelo Buonarroti.

No longer was Rome the forgotten, ruined city that Filippo had found it. Under the restored power of the Popes, she was returning to her former grandeur. Magnificent buildings were everywhere under construction.

Michelangelo had been summoned by Pope Paul III to complete the church of St. Peter, begun some time before by Donato Bramante. The cathedral was unfinished; like St. Mary of the Flower, it had no dome over the crossing. Michelangelo studied Filippo's dome as carefully as Filippo had once studied the Pantheon. He said of it:

"It would be difficult to equal . . . impossible to surpass. I shall build its sister, bigger perhaps, but not more beautiful."

And he did. His dome is like Filippo's in many ways, but particularly in its use of the upward-soaring pointed arch raised on a drum. Since then, many men have built monumental domes. London has St. Paul's Cathedral dome, built by Sir Christopher Wren at the end of the seventeenth century. Under the lovely dome, of the same period, which

St. Peter's Dome

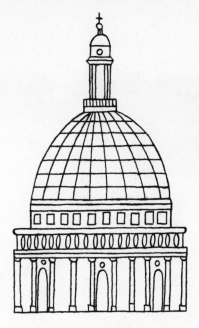

St. Paul's Dome

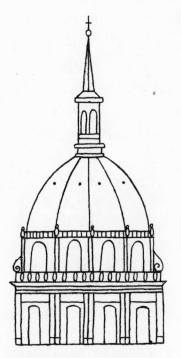

Dôme des Invalides

Capitol Dome

Jules Hardouin Mansart built for the Hôtel des Invalides in Paris, Napoleon lies buried. And, of course, in Washington we have our own familiar Capitol dome, built by Thomas Walter in the nineteenth century. And there are many more.

But, of all of these, the first was Filippo's dome.